W9-BYK-197

AN ILLUSTRATED DATA GUIDE TO

BATTLESHIPS
OF
WORLD WAR II

Compiled by
Christopher Chant

TIGER BOOKS INTERNATIONAL
LONDON

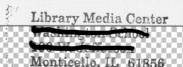

This edition published in 1997 by
Tiger Books International PLC
Twickenham

Published in Canada in 1997 by
Vanwell Publishing Limited
St. Catharines, Ontario

© Graham Beehag Books
Christchurch
Dorset

Printed and bound in Hong Kong

ISBN 1-85501-857-8

CONTENTS

'Dunkerque' class
(France)

Type: Fast battleship

Displacement: 26,500 tons standard and 35,500 tons full load

Dimensions: Length 703ft 9in (214.5m); beam 102ft 3in (31.16m); draught 28ft 6in (8.69m)

Armament: Eight 13in (330mm) guns in two quadruple turrets, sixteen 5.1in (130mm) dual-purpose guns in three quadruple and two twin turrets, eight 37mm AA guns in four twin mountings, and thirty-two 0.52in (13.2mm) AA machine-guns in eight quadruple mountings

Armour: 9.5–7.7in (240–195mm) belt, 9–3.9in (22–898mm) bulkheads, 5–4.5in (127115mm) main deck, 2–1.6in (51–40mm) lower deck; 1.6–1.2in (40–30mm) torpedo bulkheads, 13–5.9in (330–150mm) turrets, 13.6in (345mm) barbettes, 3.5–3.1in (89–80mm) secondary turrets, and 10.6in (270mm) conning tower

The Dunkerque was severely damaged in two British attacks during July 1940, but was refloated in 1942 and sailed to Toulon, where the ship was blown up in November 1942.

Propulsion: Six Indret small-tube boilers supplying steam to four sets of Parsons geared turbines delivering a total of 112,500hp (83,880kW) to four shafts

Performance: Maximum speed 29.5kt; radius 7,500nm (8,635 miles; 13,900km) at 15kt

Complement: 1,431

France

Name	Builder	Commissioned
Dunkerque	Brest Dockyard	May 1937
Strasbourg	Penhoet	Dec 1938

The first French capital ships to be laid down after the 'battleship holiday' imposed by the Washington Treaty of early 1920s, the 'Dunkerque' class fast battleships were the result of a series of design studies undertaken during the 1920s and were ultimately produced as a counter to the German 'Deutschland' class light capital ships generally known as 'pocket battleships'. As such, the 'Dunkerque' class battleships were armoured to withstand the fire of the German 11in (280mm) gun carried by the units of the 'Deutschland' class

ships, and were thus protected to a relatively light extent. Because of this fact and their high speed, they were frequently termed 'battle-cruisers'.

The design was interesting for the fact that the main armament, consisting of a new 13in (330mm) gun (a calibre considerably smaller than the maximum permitted under the terms of the Washington Treaty), was mounted in two quadruple turrets located forward of the superstructure. Although this arrangement enabled magazine protection to be concentrated, in the process saving weight and both building time and cost, it had the major disadvantage of restricting the main guns' arcs of fire (no effective fire abaft the beam was possible) and resulted in the severe risk of a single hit disabling half the main battery. The secondary armament of sixteen 5.1in (130mm) dual-purpose guns, was located in three quadruple turrets aft and two twin turrets amidships, and was based on a weapon of new calibre that proved somewhat less than successful in service. The tertiary battery comprised light weapons in two calibres optimised for the anti-aircraft role. An aircraft catapult and hangar were provided right aft, the latter providing facilities for four Loire-Nieuport LN.130 floatplanes that could be recovered with the aid of a crane from the surface of the sea.

In terms of armour protection, the main belt was of the sloped rather than vertical type, and although it was not of battleship proportions the total weight of armour that was carried comprised more than 35 per cent of the standard displacement. The underwater protection was particularly comprehensive, and included layers of rubber compound designed to be impervious to water.

The *Strasbourg* was launched in December 1936 at the Penhoet yard in St Nazaire, and differed from her sister ship only in the details of her bridge. Neither ship received significant modification during its career. The *Dunkerque* was attacked by the British on two separate occasions to prevent the possibility of her use by the Germans during World War II (1939–45), and was finally scuttled by her own crew in November 1942 at Toulon to prevent her falling into the hands of the Germans as they overran the unoccupied part of France after the Allied landing in French North-West Africa; the *Strasbourg* met a similar fate, although the ship was raised in 1945 and was used for a number of experimental purposes before being broken up in 1958.

'Richelieu' class
(France)

Type: Battleship

Displacement: 38,500 tons standard and 47,500 tons full load

Dimensions: Length 813ft 3in (247.85m); beam 108ft 9in (33.0m); draught 31ft 9in (9.63m)

Armament: Eight 15in (381mm) guns in two quadruple turrets, nine 6in (152mm) guns in three triple turrets, twelve 3.94in (100mm) AA guns in six twin turrets, sixteen 37mm AA guns in eight twin mountings, and eight 0.52in (13.2mm) AA machine-guns in single mountings

Armour: 13.6–9.8in (345–250mm) belt, 6.7–5.1in (170–130mm) main deck, 1.6in (40mm) lower deck, 16.9–6.7in (430–170mm) main turrets, 5.1–2.8in (130–70mm) secondary turrets, and 13.4in (340mm) conning tower

Propulsion: Six Indret boilers supplying steam to four sets of Loire-built Parsons (*Richelieu*) or Penhoet-built Parsons (*Jean Bart*) geared turbines delivering 155,000hp (115,570kW) to four shafts

Performance: Maximum speed 32kt; radius about 8,000nm (9,210 miles; 14,285km) at 15kt

Complement: 1,670

France		
Name	*Builder*	*Commissioned*
Richelieu	Brest Dockyard	Jun 1940
Jean Bart	Loire and Penhoet	Jan 1949

Although the two units of the 'Dunkerque' class were undoubtedly fine ships within the limitations of their gun calibre and protection, it was clear to the French naval authorities by the early 1930s that new German and Italian

The ships of the 'Richelieu' class, here epitomised by the Richelieu herself, were unique in having a main armament of eight 15in (381mm) guns located in two quadruple turrets forward of the superstructure. The secondary armament of 6in (152mm) guns were grouped in triple turrets over the rear of the ship.

construction would have to be countered with considerably heavier battleships if France were to maintain her position *vis-à-vis* these two potential enemies. The result was the 'Richelieu' class, which was designed with high speed, true battleship armament, and protection to match. The basic pattern was that of the 'Dunkerque' class, although scaled-up in this instance to provide the displacement required for the heavier armament and protection that was planned. Among the primary features retained from the 'Dunkerque' class, however, were the location of the main armament as a pair of superfiring quadruple turrets forward of the superstructure, and the grouping of the secondary armament in turrets abreast and abaft the superstructure in the area free of main armament requirements.

The main armament was the excellent new 15in (381mm) gun, which could fire a 1,940lb (880kg) shell at the rate of two rounds per minute to a range of 49,210yds (45,000m) at an elevation of 35°. Each of the quadruple turrets in fact comprised two twin mountings in a common gunhouse. The secondary armament was based on five triple 6in (152mm) turrets, three aft and two amidships in the style pioneered by the two 'Dunkerque' class battleships. At the stern of the ship were a hangar and two catapults for the operation of three Loire-Nieuport LN.130 seaplanes that were designed to alight on the water after a mission before taxiing alongside the ship for recovery by a crane.

While the *Richelieu* was building, her original arrangement of funnel amidships and control tower/mainmast aft was altered to a combined amidships unit with the top of the funnel angled back sharply to ensure that the smoke was kept clear of the tower bridge that was located farther forward.

The protection was more extensive and better arranged than that of the 'Dunkerque' class ships, and included an inclined internal belt providing a good level of protection against long-range plunging fire.

The *Richelieu* was almost complete at the time of France's armistice with Germany in the opening stages of World War II, and she escaped from Brest in north-west France (in the area occupied by the Germans) to Dakar in France's West African territory of Senegal. The ship joined the Allies in 1942, and sailed to the United States for a delayed total completion in 1943. The final disposition was much as intended in the original design, although the quarterdeck catapults and aircraft were deleted, search and fire-control radar was added, the secondary battery was restricted to the three aftermost triple turrets and, reflecting the greater threat to capital ships from aircraft after the middle of World War II, the AA armament was

The Bismarck, lead unit of a two-ship class, was well planned, excellently built, and carried a primary armament of eight 15in (381m) guns in four twin turrets, but was fatally obsolescent in some of her defensive and secondary/tertiary armament features.

augmented to 14 quadruple 40mm Bofors and 48 single 20mm Oerlikon mountings. The displacement increased by some 3,000 tons by these alterations and also by the provision of increased bunkerage for long-range operations.

In 1943 the *Richelieu* was attached to the British Home Fleet, but in 1944 and 1945 she was passed to the British Pacific Fleet. The ship finally returned to France in 1946 after a spell of duty in Indo-China. In 1956 she was put into reserve, and in 1968 she was finally scrapped.

The *Jean Bart* was built by Penhoet at St Nazaire, and the fitting out of the ship was just beginning when France fell to the Germans. Nonetheless, the ship managed to escape, reaching Casablanca in French North-West Africa in June 1940. Work on completion of the ship proceeded slowly as a result of shortages of the required armament and equipment compounded by the limited nature of the local yard, but even so, the ship fired on the American forces landing in North-West Africa in November 1942. The ship was badly damaged by the fire of an American battleship, however, and was finally completed only after World War II with a secondary battery of nine 6in (152mm) guns, and an AA armament of twenty-four 3.94in (100mm) guns in 12 twin turrets and twenty-eight 57mm guns in seven quadruple turrets. For improved protection against torpedoes, the ship was also given lateral bulges along the waterline, which increased the maximum beam to 116ft 3in (35.45m). The *Jean Bart* was scrapped in 1969.

As part of the 1938 programme another two 'Richelieu' class battleships were authorised. These were the *Clemenceau* to be built at Brest Dockyard, and the *Gascogne* to be built at St Nazaire by the Chantiers de la Loire and the Chantiers de St Nazaire-Penhoet. The *Clemenceau*'s incomplete hull was sunk in 1944 by British air attack: the ship would have differed from the first two ships of the class mainly in her secondary battery of twelve 6in (152mm) guns in two superfiring turrets aft and two turrets amidships, and would have carried no aircraft. The *Gascogne* (which was to have been built on the slip vacated by the *Jean Bart*) was never laid down, and would have differed more radically in having a fore-and-aft arrangement of the two quadruple main-armament turrets, a centreline disposition for the secondary armament of nine 6in (152mm) guns in three triple turrets, and an augmented anti-aircraft battery sixteen 3.94in (100mm) guns in eight twin turrets, and twenty 37mm guns in two quadruple and six twin mountings.

'Bismarck' class
(Germany)

Type: Battleship

Displacement: 41,675 tons standard and 50,155 tons full load

Dimensions: Length 823ft 6in (251.0m); beam 118ft 1in (36.0m); draught 29ft 6in (9.0m)

Armament: Eight 15in (381mm) guns in four twin turrets, twelve 5.9in (150mm) guns in six twin turrets, sixteen 4.1in (105mm) AA guns in eight twin turrets, sixteen 37mm AA guns in eight twin mountings, and twelve 20mm AA cannon in single mountings

Armour: 12.6–5.7in (320–145mm) belt, 8.7–1.75in (220–45mm) bulkheads, 4.7–1.2in (120–30mm) decks, 8.7in (220mm) barbettes, 14.1–5.1in (360–130mm) main turrets, 3.9–0.8in (100–20mm) secondary turrets, 13.8–1.2in (350–30mm) conning tower

Propulsion: 12 Wagner boilers supplying steam to three sets of Blohm & Voss geared turbines delivering 150,170hp (111,965kW) to three shafts

Performance: Maximum speed 30.1kt; radius 8,800nm (10,250 miles; 16,500km) at 17kt

Complement: 2,092

Germany		
Name	Builder	Commissioned
Bismarck	Blohm & Voss	Aug 1940
Tirpitz	Wilhelmshaven	Feb 1941

The first large battleships built for Germany's new navy, after the accession to power of Adolf Hitler and his subsequent abrogation of the military limitations imposed upon Germany by the Treaty of Versailles in 1919, were two

35,000-ton battleships. As with the two earlier battle-cruisers of the 'Gneisenau' class, the design of these battleships closely followed the final German capital ship designs of World War I, although considerably revised in features such as greater installed power for higher speed. The first of this pair of ships was launched and christened *Bismarck* in February 1939, and this impressive vessel was 6,000 tons heavier than permitted by international treaty limit, although much of the extra tonnage was accounted for by additional fuel bunkerage rather than heavier armament and armour.

The gap between the design and construction of major warships forced upon Germany by the Treaty of Versailles meant that, while the other major naval powers such as the UK, the USA and Japan had been able to experiment with older or redundant ships to assess the capabilities of modern shells and the level of protection afforded by improved armour, Germany had been denied this opportunity. Another advantage that was denied to Germany was the process of continued capital ship development. Nevertheless, theoretical work had continued in secret, and when the provisions of the Anglo-German Naval Treaty of 1935 were implemented, the Germans were well placed to move ahead with the design of two of the three 35,000-ton battleships permitted by the treaty. The 'battleship holiday' imposed on Germany dictated that the basic design of the World War I 'Baden' class of super-dreadnought battleship was re-used for the hull, but the overall design was considerably revised to

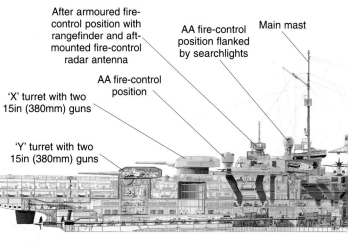

After armoured fire-control position with rangefinder and aft-mounted fire-control radar antenna

AA fire-control position flanked by searchlights

Main mast

AA fire-control position

'X' turret with two 15in (380mm) guns

'Y' turret with two 15in (380mm) guns

cater for the 6kt increase in speed demanded for modern naval operations, with radically improved underwater protection and enhanced anti-aircraft armament: the overall length was increased and the length/beam ratio was reduced from 6.04/1 to 6.71/1.

What cannot be denied, however, is that the re-use of a basic design from World War I meant the retention of several potentially deadly flaws: the rudders and steering gear had only poor protection, while the location of the main armoured deck toward the lower edge of the belt (at a time when other major powers had shifted it toward the upper edge of the belt) left most of the ship's communications and data-transmission systems exposed to the plunging fire associated with the modern type of long-range gun engagement. Both these features were crucial in the loss of the *Bismarck*. A further design deficiency resulted from Germany's lack of research into dual-purpose secondary gun batteries: additional displacement had to be provided for separate low-angle (anti-ship) and high-angle (anti-aircraft) batteries of 5.9in (150mm) and 4.1in (105mm) weapons respectively. Another fault, although one that was little appreciated at the time, was the indifferent quality of the armour in comparison with that of countries which had been able to undertake destructive tests of World War I capital ships. While the *Bismarck*'s conning tower was theoretically armoured against 15in (381mm) shell fire, in the event it was penetrated by British 8in (203mm) rounds. A final failing was the indifferent quality of the German 15in (381mm) shells, of which a high proportion did not detonate correctly.

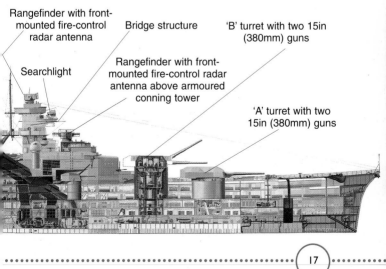

Rangefinder with front-mounted fire-control radar antenna

Bridge structure

'B' turret with two 15in (380mm) guns

Searchlight

Rangefinder with front-mounted fire-control radar antenna above armoured conning tower

'A' turret with two 15in (380mm) guns

For all her faults, however, the *Bismarck* was a fine ship with a number of good points: she was very strongly built, which made her very difficult to sink; her fire-control systems (especially those for the HA armament) were excellent; she was fitted with gunnery radar at a time when this was a rarity in the capital ships of most other navies; and for her main role of commerce-raiding she was both well planned and well built.

For the main armament and the low-angle secondary armament used against surface targets there were three separate directors each in the forward and after command positions, while the command post in the foretop had four directors for the simultaneous control of both batteries. Provision was also made for the carriage of up to six reconnaissance and gunnery-spotting seaplanes.

The *Bismarck* was commissioned in August 1940 and underwent eight months of training in the Baltic before she was considered ready for a breakout into the Atlantic on a commerce-raiding cruise. In May 1941, she and the heavy cruiser *Prinz Eugen* sailed from the Baltic bound for Bergen on the west coast of Norway, but the two ships' passage from the Baltic had been detected by pro-British Swedes and the Admiralty had been alerted by analysis of radio traffic. As a result the heavy cruiser *Suffolk* was already on station in the Denmark Strait, between Iceland and Greenland, and on 23 May she detected the two German ships on radar. During the morning of the following day the chasing Battle-Cruiser Squadron of British ships sought to intercept the German vessels, but the German ships got the range quickly: shells from the *Prinz Eugen* started a fire aboard the battle-cruiser *Hood*, which blew up shortly after this, whilst shells from the *Bismarck* hit the bridge of the battleship *Prince of Wales*, which was then ordered to break off the action, leaving the German ships to continue their southward progress into the Atlantic.

Examination of the *Bismarck*'s bunkers revealed that a large quantity of fuel had been contaminated by underwater damage, and Admiral Günther Lütjens decided to forget his primary commerce-raiding task, and headed for Brest. During that night Fairey Swordfish torpedo bombers from the aircraft carrier *Victorious* attacked with torpedoes, but the single hit inflicted only minor damage. For a while the *Bismarck* eluded her pursuers, but after unwisely transmitting a long radio signal she was detected on 26 May, and that night, Swordfish bombers from the aircraft carrier *Ark Royal* hit her with two torpedoes, one of which caused major damage to the German battleship's steering gear.

There followed unsuccessful attacks by British destroyers, but the *Bismarck* was doomed, unable to manoeuvre and steaming at only 5kt. On the next morning the battleships *King George V* and *Rodney* came over the northern horizon, and at 08.41 opened a deadly fire. By 09.20 the *Bismarck* had been silenced: in this 39-minute period the German ship had scored only one 'straddle' on the *Rodney* and had hit her with a few splinters. In the final stages of the battle the range came down to only 4,000yds (3,660m), and the *Bismarck* was battered into a drifting wreck that was finally torpedoed by the light cruiser *Dorsetshire* to sink at 10.40.

Completed in February 1941, the *Tirpitz* initially differed from the *Bismarck* only in her greater power and range, but later modifications included the addition of twenty-four 21in (533mm) torpedo tubes in eight triple mountings and the incorporation of a light anti-aircraft battery of fifty-eight 20mm cannon. The ship was based for most of her career in Norwegian waters, posing a severe threat to Allied convoys plying the Arctic route to the USSR's northern ports, but the ship was damaged by British midget-submarine attack and was finally sunk by air attack in November 1944.

The Bismarck was a good seaboat with first-class performance, but while an adequate warship in most respects of armament and protection had a number of poor design features such as lack of full protection for the steering gear.

'Hood' class
(UK)

Type: Battle-cruiser revised to battleship standard

Displacement: 41,200 tons standard and 44,600 tons full load

Dimensions: Length 860ft 7in (262.8m); beam 105ft 2.5in (34.5m); draught 31ft 6in (9.6m)

Armament: Eight 15in (381mm) guns in four twin turrets, twelve 5.5in (140mm) guns in single mountings, four 4in (102mm) AA guns in single mountings, and six 21in (533mm) torpedo tubes in two triple mountings

Armour: 12–5in (305–127mm) belt, 5–4in (127–102mm) bulkheads, 3–1in (76–25mm) decks, 12–5in (305–127mm) barbettes, 15–5in (381–127mm) main turrets, and 11–3in (279–76mm) conning tower

Propulsion: 24 Yarrow boilers supplying steam to four sets of Brown-Curtis geared turbines delivering 151,280hp (112,795kW) to four shafts

Performance: Maximum speed 32.1kt; radius 5,200nm (5,990 miles; 9,635km) at 18kt

Complement: 1,169

UK		
Name	Builder	Commissioned
Hood	John Brown & Co.	Mar 1920

When it became clear in 1915 that the Germans were preparing the 'Mackensen' class of battle-cruisers with 15in (381mm) guns, the British decided to reply with a new battle-cruiser class featuring the very latest ideas in speed, armament and protection, and in this respect the designers were aided by the relaxation in World War I of the previous rule that tied capital ship dimensions to those of existing drydocks. Great attention went into the design of the *Hood* by E.L. Attwood and S.V. Goodall, for it was not until 1916 that suitable slips would become available, and this gave considerable latitude for the finalisation of a design for a ship with armament superior to that of the two units of the 'Renown' battle-cruiser class and with protection superior to that of the single unit of the 'Tiger' battle-cruiser class.

What emerged, therefore, was a ship with the same armament as the 'Queen Elizabeth' class super-dreadnought battleships in combination with greater speed as a result of greater power but, most unfortunately, less protection. Orders were placed in April 1916 for a total of four ships: the *Hood* was to be built by John Brown, *Anson* by Armstrongs, *Howe* by Cammell Laird, and *Rodney* by Fairfield. Three of the ships had been ordered before the Battle of Jutland was fought in June 1916, and even the

The Hood was the most popular warship of the Royal Navy with the British public in the years between the world wars, but while a patently effective ship in offensive terms was revealed in the first part of World War II to possess wholly inadequate protection.

preliminary assessments of the damage suffered by the British ships caused a radical review of the design: the battle-cruiser concept was abandoned, and the design was revised. When it was learned that the Germans had ceased work on the 'Mackensen' class battle-cruisers, all the ships but the *Hood* were cancelled in October 1918.

The *Hood* finally appeared in 1920 as a monumentally impressive ship of very elegant line, and one that was immediately taken to the hearts of the British public. As a fighting ship the *Hood* was a mixture of old and new: on the one hand she was the last British capital ship with an open secondary battery and mast-head tops for control, but on the other hand she had an inclined armour belt, a main battery whose guns could be elevated to a high angle for maximum possible range, small-tube boilers permitting the development of some 30 per cent more power than the 'Renown' class ships for the same weight, and a secondary battery based on the new 5.5in (140mm) gun.

The main armament was accommodated in four centreline twin turrets (two forward and two aft in superfiring pairs) and had an elevation of 20°; this was later increased to 30° when an assessment of the fighting at Jutland revealed that battle ranges were increasing rapidly. At the same time, open sighting hoods were replaced by rangefinders, each turret having its own 30ft (9.14m) unit. The 5.5in (140mm) secondary armament was typical of its period, however, and the location of this battery's weapons, in five open positions on each forecastle deck beam and two on the shelter deck, was completely obsolete: none of the mountings could be trained aft of the beam, and the four 5.5in (140mm) guns originally intended for this quarter's defence had been deleted in order to save weight.

The *Hood*'s armour arrangement was typical of its period, with the main weight of armour concentrated against low-angle fire but slightly modified with extra

A fine ship at the time of her conception as a fast battle-cruiser, the Hood was well armed and fast, but during the 1930s was rebuilt (as were many of her counterparts in Japan), and the result was her loss to the type of long-range plunging fire that her protective scheme had not been designed to counter.

horizontal protection against high-angle fire and bombs. The belt was angled outward to worsen the impact angle of any incoming shell. Waterline bulges were fitted for protection against torpedoes, and these bulges were filled with tubes to help absorb shock in the event of a torpedo strike.

Little was done in the way of modifications before World War II, when the *Hood* had her AA armament increased. The ship was due to undergo a major reconstruction and modernisation starting in 1939, but this programme never began, and the ship blew up after being hit by a salvo from the *Bismarck* on 24 May 1941, only three of her complement surviving.

'Nelson' class
(UK)

Type: Battleship

Displacement: 33,950 tons standard and 38,000 tons full load

Dimensions: Length 710ft 0in (216.8m); beam 106ft 0in (32.4m); draught 31ft 6in (9.6m)

Armament: Nine 16in (406mm) guns in three triple turrets, twelve 6in (152mm) guns in six twin turrets, six 4.7in (119mm) AA guns in single mountings, and two 24.5in (622mm) torpedo tubes

Armour: 14–13in (356–330mm) belt, 14–12in (356–305mm) bulkheads, 6.25–3in (159–76mm) decks, 15–14in (381–356mm) barbettes, 16–7in (406–178mm) turrets, 15–1in (381–25mm) secondary turrets, and 16in (406mm) conning tower

Propulsion: Eight Admiralty boilers supplying steam to two Brown-Curtis geared turbines delivering 45,000hp (33,550kW) to two shafts

Performance: Maximum speed 23.5kt; radius 14,300nm (16,465 miles; 26,500km) at 12kt

Complement: 1,314

UK		
Name	*Builder*	*Commissioned*
Nelson	Vickers-Armstrong	Jun 1927
Rodney	Cammell Laird	Aug 1927

The *Nelson* and her sister ship *Rodney* were the first battleships completed in accordance with the principles

The Rodney with her sister ship Nelson had an exemplary main armament of nine 16in (406mm) guns in three triple turrets and was very well protected, but paid for these advantages in a low-powered propulsion arrangement.

ordained in the Washington Treaty of 1922, which fixed maxima of 35,000 tons for displacement and 16in (406mm) for main armament calibre. The designers, E.L. Attwood and S.V. Goodall, therefore faced a difficult task in designing the pair of ships that the UK was permitted, to balance the Japanese 'Nagato' and American 'Maryland' classes, whose ships had 16in (406mm) guns. What emerged from this process was a scaled-down version of the 'G3' battle-cruiser design planned in 1921, with the same armament and level of protection but, as a result of treaty displacement limitations, with a reduction in the hull volume covered by the armour and the installation of considerably less powerful machinery. The need to economise on the area of armour also dictated the disposition of all three turrets forward of the tower bridge, instead of two forward and one aft as planned for the 'G3' class battle-cruisers.

Other notable features of the 'Nelson' class design were the fact that it was the only British capital ship type with

16in (406mm) guns, and also the first to have triple turrets, a secondary battery in turrets rather than main-deck casemates, a tower bridge, and its engine rooms forward of the boiler rooms (in an unsuccessful attempt to ensure that the bridge was generally clear of smoke). The 'Nelson' class battleships were also the last capital ships with separate conning towers capped by armoured and revolving director control positions.

The main turret disposition did achieve its objective of reducing the quantity of armour needed, but also made fire abaft the beam impossible because of the damage that would be caused to the superstructure by the guns' enormous blast pattern. The 'A', 'B' and 'C' turrets each mounted a trio of 16in (406mm) guns, each weighing 103.5 tons and firing a 2,461lb (1,116kg) shell with a muzzle velocity of 2,953ft (900m) per second to a range of 35,000yds (32,005m) at an elevation of 40°, which also made it possible for the main armament to be used against distant aircraft. The secondary armament was grouped toward the stern, and was disposed in six twin turrets that were, for the first time in any Royal Navy warship, of the power-operated type. The AA armament was located abreast and abaft the tower bridge, and was later considerably strengthened: by the end of World War II, the *Nelson*'s AA armament comprised six 4.7in (119mm), forty-eight 2pdr, sixteen 40mm Bofors and sixty-one 20mm Oerlikon weapons.

Only the vital areas (waterline, turrets, magazines, barbettes, machinery spaces and conning tower) were armoured against the main-calibre guns of any likely opponent. The disposition and thickness of the armour was very good in both the vertical and horizontal planes, and formed an intrinsic part of the ship's structure. However, it was clear by the beginning of World War II that the pace of warplane development had been so great since the design of the 'Nelson' class, that the horizontal armour could in fact be penetrated by bombs.

The feature in which most was sacrificed to meet the limitations of the Washington Treaty was power, which was about equal to that of 1,500-ton British destroyers of the period. The effect of this limitation was therefore a very low maximum speed, and both ships were noted for their bad rolling characteristics and slow response to the helm. However, both ships performed with considerable distinction in World War II, and were scrapped in 1948 and 1949 respectively.

ᅟ

ᅟ

'King George V' class
(UK)

Type: Battleship

Displacement: 38,000 tons standard and 41,460 tons full load

Dimensions: Length 745ft 0in (227.1m); beam 103ft 0in (31.4m); draught 34ft 6in (10.5m)

Armament: Ten 14in (356mm) guns in two quadruple turrets and one twin turret, sixteen 5.25in (133mm) dual-purpose guns in eight twin turrets, forty-eight 2pdr AA guns, and ten 40mm Bofors AA guns

Armour: 15–4.5in (381–114mm) belt, 11in (279mm) bulkheads, 6–5in (152–127mm) decks, 13–11in (330–279mm) barbettes, 13–6in (330–152mm) main turrets, 1.5–1in (38–25mm) secondary turrets, and 4.5in (114mm) conning tower

Propulsion: Eight Admiralty boilers supplying steam to four sets of Parsons geared turbines delivering 110,000hp (82,015kW) to four shafts

Performance: Maximum speed 29.25kt; radius 13,000nm (14,970 miles; 24,090km) at 10kt

Complement: 1,640

UK		
Name	Builder	Commissioned
King George V	Vickers-Armstrong	Dec 1940
Anson	Swan Hunter	Jun 1942
Duke of York	John Brown	Nov 1941
Howe	Fairfield	Aug 1942
Prince of Wales	Cammell Laird	Mar 1941

During the period in which the construction of battleships was limited to vessels conforming to maxima that included

The five units of the 'King George V' class, seen here in the form of the name ship, were the last series-built British battleships and offered a very good combination of firepower, protection and speed in an eminently seaworthy hull design.

35,000 tons in displacement and 16in (406mm) in the calibre of the main armament, there had been several British design exercises to test the practical limitations resulting from the Washington Treaty of 1922. In 1934 the British began to plan for a new class of battleship to be laid down in their 1936 construction programme. These ships were designed within the limits of the Washington Treaty, and were initially planned as ships with a modest speed and a main armament of nine 15in (381mm) guns in three triple turrets complemented by a secondary battery of 6in (152mm) weapons. Continued development of the design in 1934 replaced the 6in (152mm) guns with 4.7in (119mm) weapons, but these obsolescent guns were soon overtaken by the excellent 5.25in (133mm) dual-purpose gun in the type of twin turret recently introduced by the 'Dido' class light cruisers.

In 1936 the London Naval Treaty fixed a maximum calibre of 14in (356mm) unless a signatory of the Washington Treaty objected, and the design was thereupon recast for this weapon. Although there appeared every likelihood that the Treaty would not be ratified, by Japan at least, the British were faced with a problem as the gun mountings had to be ordered by mid-1936 if the first two ships were to be ready by 1940, when it was possible that the UK could be at war with Germany. In these circumstances, the Admiralty decided to ignore the general demand for a primary armament of 16in (406mm) guns and chose to retain the 14in (356mm) weapons already ordered. The Admiralty was confirmed in this decision by an analysis that indicated that this would give the ships a good balance of firepower and protection in combination with high speed. Even so, fears that the 16in (406mm) gun would in fact return were reflected in the revision of the armour to provide protection against this calibre of projectile.

The ships of this important class were initially planned

with a main armament of nine 14in (356mm) guns in three triple turrets, yielding a broadside weight of 19,080lb (8,655kg) over a maximum range of 36,000yds (32,920m), but tests against 16in (406mm) rounds showed that extra horizontal protection was required. As a result, two of the guns in the superfiring 'B' turret were sacrificed to permit the installation of more armour. The main armament was finally fixed as two quadruple turrets, forward and aft, plus a superfiring twin turret forward.

The protection was planned on the principle pioneered in the preceding 'Nelson' class battleships. Whereas the 'Nelson' class ships had featured an internal sloping belt, however, the 'King George V' class ships had a vertical external belt, continued assessments of the threat faced by these ships having suggested that repairs to an internal belt would be extremely difficult to implement. By comparison with that of the 'Nelson' class ships, the belt of the 'King George V' class ships was 1in (25mm) thicker over the magazines. The designer, Sir Arthur Johns, also deepened the belt below the waterline, as tests with the *Baden* (surrendered by the Germans at the end of World War I) had revealed that many capital ships were extremely vulnerable to the type of plunging fire that had become increasingly common as the range of ship-versus-ship engagements lengthened. Johns also raised the main horizontal armour by one deck, which was basically what the Americans and the Japanese had done in their latest battleships, but removed the external waterline bulge. Protection against the torpedo and mine was therefore vested in the double bottom, which was an internal 2in (51mm) longitudinal bulkhead with two watertight compartments sandwiching an oil-filled compartment that took up the space between the longitudinal bulkhead and the hull on each side.

The 'King George V' class battleship was a good gun platform, and the ships of the class also possessed markedly better rolling characteristics than the two units of the 'Nelson' class. Conversely, however, the design took a lot of water over the bows in any sort of sea, severely affecting speed in these adverse conditions. Some early problems were suffered with the 14in (356mm) gun mountings and with elements of the auxiliary systems (especially power for the anti-aircraft guns and pumps), but in overall terms the 'King George V' class design, evolved by W.G. Sanders and H.S. Pengelly under the supervision of Sir Arthur Johns, was highly successful.

Early in their service lives in World War II, when the threat

The King George V was completed in December 1940 and had a highly active operational career during World War II, when she served in home waters, the Arctic, the Mediterranean and finally the Pacific before being decommissioned in December 1949 and scrapped in 1958.

posed by air attack intensified rapidly, the ships received sixteen 20mm Oerlikon cannon to provide an enhanced anti-aircraft defence that was later boosted by the installation of 2pdr pom-pom weapons and 40mm Bofors guns.

The success of the ships is revealed by even the most cursory listing of their service in World War II. The *King George V* served in home waters, the Atlantic, the Mediterranean and the Pacific before being scrapped in 1957. The *Prince of Wales* served in home waters and the Atlantic before being allocated to the Far East, where she was sunk by Japanese air attack on 10 December 1941. The *Duke of York* served in the Home Fleet throughout World War II and was scrapped in 1958. The *Anson* served in home waters and in the Pacific before being scrapped in 1957, and the *Howe* served in home waters, the Mediterranean, the Arctic, the Indian Ocean and the Pacific before being scrapped in 1958.

'Cavour' class
(Italy)

Type: Battleship

Displacement: 23,090 tons standard and 25,085 tons full load

Dimensions: Length 577ft 9in (176.1m); beam 91ft 10in (28.0m); draught 30ft 10in (9.4m)

Armament: Thirteen 12in (305mm) guns in three triple and two twin turrets, eighteen 4.7in (119mm) guns in single mountings, thirteen 3in (76mm) guns in single mountings, and 17.7in (450mm) torpedo tubes

Armour: 9.8–5.1in (250–130mm) belt, 11in (279mm) turrets, 9.4in (239mm) barbettes, 5.1–4.3in (130–109mm) casemates, 1.7in (43mm) decks, and 11in (279mm) conning tower

Propulsion: 20 Blechhynden boilers supplying steam to

three sets of Yarrow turbines delivering 31,000hp
(23,115kW) to four shafts

Performance: Maximum speed 21.5kt; radius 4,800nm
(5,530 miles; 8,880km) at 10kt

Complement: 1,197

Italy		
Name	Builder	Commissioned
Conte di Cavour	La Spezia	Apr 1915
Guilio Cesare	Ansaldo	May 1914

Designed in 1908 by Engineer General Edoardo Masdea, the
three dreadnought battleships of the 'Cavour' class
represented an improvement on the all-round firepower of
the preceding *Dante Alighieri* by mounting thirteen 12in

Although built largely before World War I to an improved 'dreadnought' type design, the Conte di
Cavour *was refitted in the mid-1920s and then rebuilt in the mid-1930s to re-emerge as a
comparatively modern ship with a primary armament of ten 12.6in (320mm) guns.*

(305mm) guns in five centreline turrets (two triple turrets and two superfiring twin turrets fore and aft, and one triple turret amidships). The secondary armament arrangement of the *Dante Alighieri*, which had eight of her 4.7in (119mm) guns in twin turrets, was replaced by a casemated arrangement one deck higher.

The armament layout was certainly better than that of the *Dante Alighieri*, but this advance was offset by the fact that construction of the 'Cavour' class battleships took too long, and the ships therefore appeared only when other navies had switched to 13.5–14in (343–356mm) main guns. As evident in other Italian major warships, moreover, protection took second place to firepower and speed, although the 'Cavour' class ships' designed speed of 22kt was seldom achieved in service.

The *Leonardo da Vinci*, completed at Sestri Ponente in May 1914, sank in Taranto during August 1916 after a magazine explosion. The wreck was salvaged in September 1919 but was then sold for scrapping in March 1923 before work had begun on a reconstruction planned with a main armament of ten 12in (305mm) guns and a tertiary battery of six 4in (102mm) AA guns.

The two surviving units of the 'Cavour' class were completely redesigned in the early 1930s under the supervision of Engineer General Francesco Rotundi: the *Conte di Cavour* was rebuilt between October 1933 and June 1937, and the *Guilio Cesare* was rebuilt between October 1933 and October 1937. The improved standard to which the ships now conformed for service in World War II included a new propulsion arrangement (geared turbines delivering 93,000hp/69,340kW to two shafts for a maximum speed of 28kt), improved protection, and a completely revised armament disposition. In this last revision, the central triple turret and the casemated guns of the secondary battery were eliminated and the armament therefore included a main battery of ten 12.6in (320mm) guns as in the 'Duilio' class, a secondary battery of twelve 4.7in (119mm) guns on the forecastle deck amidships, and a tertiary battery of eight 3.9in (100mm) AA guns and about 20 smaller AA guns.

The *Conte di Cavour* was sunk by a British air-launched torpedo attack at Taranto in November 1940. The *Guilio Cesare* survived World War II and was handed over to the USSR as part of Italy's war reparations in 1948, and served in the Black Sea as the *Novorossiysk* until late 1955.

'Duilio' class
(Italy)

Type: Battleship

Displacement: 22,695 tons standard and 25,200 tons full load

Dimensions: Length 577ft 9in (176.1m); beam 91ft 10in (28.0m); draught 29ft 2in (8.9m)

Armament: Thirteen 12in (305mm) guns in three triple and two twin turrets, sixteen 6in (152mm) guns in single mountings, eighteen 3in (76mm) guns in single mountings, and 17.7in (450mm) torpedo tubes

Armour: 9.8–5.1in (250–130mm) belt, 9.4in (239mm) turrets and barbettes, 5in (127mm) casemates, 1.6in (40mm) decks, and 12.6in (320mm) conning tower

Propulsion: 20 Yarrow boilers supplying steam to three sets of Yarrow turbines delivering 32,000hp (23,860kW) to three shafts

Performance: Maximum speed 21.5kt; radius 4,800nm (5,530 miles; 8,880km) at 10kt

Complement: 1,233

Italy		
Name	Builder	Commissioned
Caio Duilio	Castellammare	May 1915
Andrea Doria	La Spezia	Mar 1916

As completed in the first part of World War I, the *Caio Duilio* and the *Andrea Doria* were basically developments of the preceding 'Cavour' class dreadnought battleships, with a secondary armament of casemated 6in (152mm) rather than 4.7in (119mm) guns. The increased topweight of this heavier battery could have presented stability problems, so the midships secondary battery of the 'Cavour' class was split into two groups fore and aft of amidships and the central 12in (305mm) triple turret was located one deck lower. The tripod forward mast was also before rather than abaft the fore funnel. A designed speed of 22kt could only be achieved with some 10,000hp (7,455kW) more than the designed output of the propulsion arrangement with its combination of coal- and oil-fired boilers, and the level of protection (especially below the waterline where only protective coal bunkers were fitted) was decidedly poor.

After extensive reconstruction in 1937–40 to the plans of Engineer General Francesco Rotundi, the two units were in effect new ships. The main changes were centred on an increase of 35ft 6in (10.8m) in overall length with a completely remodelled bow, a superstructure modelled on that of the *Vittorio Veneto*, and a new propulsion arrangement with eight oil-fired boilers supplying steam to geared steam turbines delivering 85,000hp (63,375kW) to two shafts for a maximum speed of 27kt. Protection over the machinery and magazines was improved dramatically and 1.6in (40mm) anti-torpedo bulkheads were fitted. The armament was also altered to a standard that included ten 12.6in (320mm) guns: the central triple turret had been removed, and the guns in the remaining turrets (a balanced fore-and-aft arrangement with two triple turrets and two superfiring twin turrets) had been bored out to the larger calibre. The remainder of the armament included a secondary armament of twelve 5.3in (135mm) guns in four triple turrets, and a tertiary battery of ten 3.6in (91mm) AA guns in single mountings supplemented by about 30 smaller-calibre AA weapons.

Both ships were deployed mainly for convoy interception or escort during the course of Italy's adherence to the Axis cause in World War II, when the *Caio Duilio* was out of action for six months in 1940 after taking a torpedo hit. The two ships were finally scrapped in 1957–58.

'Vittorio Veneto' class
(Italy)

Type: Battleship

Displacement: 41,375 tons standard and 45,750 tons full load

Dimensions: Length 778ft 8in (237.8m); beam 107ft 9.5in (32.9m); draught 31ft 5in (9.6m)

Armament: Nine 15in (381mm) guns in three triple turrets, twelve 6in (152mm) guns in four triple turrets, four 4.7in (119mm) guns in single mountings, twelve 3.5in (89mm) AA guns in single mountings, twenty 37mm AA guns, and thirty-two 20mm AA cannon

Armour: 13.8–2.4in (350–61mm) belt, 8.1–1.4in (205–35mm) decks, 13.8in (350mm) barbettes, 13.8–3.9in (350–100mm) turrets, and 5.9–4in (150–102mm) secondary turrets, and 10in (254mm) conning tower

Propulsion: Eight Yarrow boilers supplying steam to four sets of Belluzzo geared turbines delivering 134,615hp (100,370kW) to four shafts

Performance: Maximum speed 31.4kt; radius 4,000nm (4,605 miles; 7,400km) at 16kt

Complement: 1,861

Italy		
Name	Builder	Commissioned
Vittorio Veneto	CRDA	Apr 1940
Littorio	Ansaldo	May 1940
Roma	CRDA	Jun 1942

When France refused to ratify the London Naval Agreement and started to build the two fast battleships of the 'Dunkerque' class, the combination of security requirements and nationalist pride left Italy with little real alternative but the construction of two superior battleships. As a result,

orders were placed for two units of a design originally drawn up in 1928. This first pair of battleships comprised the *Vittorio Veneto* and the *Littorio* to be built by CRDA and Ansaldo respectively. The original design displacement was 35,000 tons, but when the ships were launched this had increased to a standard displacement of 41,500 tons.

The two ships were particularly impressive in the water as they combined an aggressive overall appearance with the elegance of line typical of most Italian warships designed after World War I. The sole inharmonious feature of the design was the high position of the after 15in (381mm) turret, which was dictated by the Italians' desire to locate unhangared aircraft on the quarterdeck, where they would have been vulnerable to blast damage from main-calibre guns in a lower position. The nine 15in (381mm) guns were located in three triple turrets installed in a centreline arrangement with a superfiring pair forward and a single unit aft. The secondary armament was based on twelve 6in (152mm) guns in four triple turrets: pairs of these turrets were installed abreast 'B' and 'X' turrets. The tertiary armament was based on twelve 3.5in (89mm) AA guns in single mountings installed as six on each beam, and four 4.7in (119mm) guns in single mountings installed as pairs on the forecastle deck amidships and outboard of the 3.5in (89mm) gun mountings. Lighter weapons, including 37mm guns and 20mm cannon for the anti-aircraft task, were dotted about the superstructure and upper works.

The armour protection was indifferent by comparison with that of contemporary battleships as a result of the

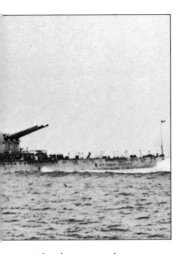

The Vittorio Veneto was an attractive battleship typical of design practices in the early 1930s, and offered a good combination of firepower, protection and speed, although experience in World War II revealed deficiencies in protection against bombing attacks.

Italian preference for speed and agility to evade serious damage. Thin and shallow, the main belt covered only the area from a point forward of 'A' turret to a point aft of 'X' turret. Thinner armour extended to the bows and stern, and also covered the sides between the turrets as far up as the forecastle deck. The poorest feature of the protective scheme was the horizontal armour which, as events were to prove in the course of World War II, could not withstand the type of bomb increasingly used in the war.

The *Vittorio Veneto* and the *Littorio* were each built with a slightly curved stem, but after initial trials were revised with a straight stem, which increased overall length by 5ft 11in (1.8m) and allowed the greater flare that provided a drier forecastle.

The *Vittorio Veneto* suffered torpedo damage on two occasions during 1941, and was also damaged by bombs in 1943 before the Italian surrender. The ship then spent the rest of the war in the Bitter Lakes region of the Suez Canal, was allocated to the UK as part of Italy's war reparations in 1946, and was scrapped between 1948 and 1950. The *Littorio* was completed one week after the *Vittorio Veneto*. The ship suffered very extensive damage during the British air raid on Taranto in November 1940, and it was mid-1941 before she rejoined the Italian fleet. She was hit on two occasions by bombs, and on a third by a torpedo before being renamed *Italia* in June 1943. The ship was badly damaged by a German guided bomb while steaming to surrender in Malta during September 1943, and was scrapped between 1948 and 1950.

Two other units of the class were ordered from the same yards in 1938: the *Impero* was never completed after being launched in November 1939, and the *Roma* was completed in June 1942 but was sunk by a German glide bomb on 9 September 1943.

'Fuso' class
(Japan)

Type: Battleship

Displacement: 30,600 tons standard and 35,900 tons full load

Dimensions: Length 673ft 0in (205.1m); beam 94ft 0in (28.65m); draught 28ft 3in (8.61m)

Armament: Twelve 14in (356mm) guns in six twin turrets, sixteen 6in (152mm) guns in single mountings, four 3.1in (80mm) AA guns in single mountings, and six 21in (533mm) torpedo tubes in single mountings

Armour: 12–4in (305–102mm) belt and bulkheads, 12–4.5in (305–114mm) turrets, 8in (203mm) barbettes, 6in (152mm) casemates, 2–1.25in (51–32mm) deck, 13.75–5.3in (349–135mm) conning tower

Propulsion: 24 Miyabara boilers supplying steam to four sets of Brown-Curtis turbines delivering 40,000hp (29,825kW) to four shafts

Performance: Maximum speed 23kt; radius 8,000nm (9,210 miles; 14,800km) at 14kt

Complement: 1,193

Japan		
Name	*Builder*	*Commissioned*
Fuso	Kure NY	Nov 1915
Yamashiro	Yokosuka NY	Mar 1917

Built in Japanese yards to a Japanese design, and originally to have been complemented by another pair of dreadnought battleships that were later redesigned to appear as the 'Ise' class, these ships fully confirmed the appearance of Japan as a major naval power, especially in the Pacific Ocean: the two Japanese units had greater gun power than the USA's 'Texas' and 'Oklahoma' class battleships and matched the later 'Pennsylvania' class battleships, although the Japanese ships had poorer protection and were considerably longer than their American counterparts. Two benefits of the greater length, however, were the reduced chance of a single hit destroying or incapacitating one quarter of any ship's major firepower and, as a result of their finer length/beam ratio, the ships' greater maximum speed, which was 2kt faster than that of the 'Pennsylvania' class ships.

The main-calibre guns were based on the 14in (356mm) mountings supplied by the British for the 'Kongo' class battle-cruisers, but for the first time in a major Japanese warship they were of indigenous design and manufacture.

The Yamashiro was built as an improved 'dreadnought' before World War I, but was rebuilt radically during the early 1930s to re-emerge as a powerfully armed and well-protected ship that finally succumbed to shellfire and three torpedo hits in the Battle of Leyte Gulf during October 1944.

The third turret was carried, in a unique arrangement, at forecastle deck level between the funnels, and the fourth turret was installed one deck higher in a position abaft the second funnel.

In 1927–28 both of the 'Fuso' class battleships underwent an extensive refit, in the course of which both ships were given built-up foremasts and two 3.1in (80mm) AA guns. The two ships were rebuilt between 1930 and 1935, emerging with huge and visually impressive so-called 'pagoda' foremasts replacing the forward funnel, built-up main masts, considerably enhanced deck and underwater protection (armour weight increased from 8,588 to 12,199 tons), and hulls lengthened aft for an overall length of 698ft 0in (212.75m). At the same time, the propulsion arrangement was replaced by a new machinery outfit comprising six oil-fired boilers supplying steam to four sets of Kanpon geared steam turbines delivering 75,000hp (55,920kW) to four shafts for a maximum speed of 24.7kt and a radius of 11,000nm (12,665 miles; 20,350km) at 16kt. The main armament remained unaltered, but revision of the other elements of the armament included the alteration of the secondary armament to fourteen 6in (152mm) guns in single turrets, and of the tertiary armament to eight 5in (127mm) dual-purpose guns in four twin turrets and sixteen 25mm AA guns in eight twin mountings, increased to 37 such weapons by mid-1944. Provision was also made for floatplanes.

Late in 1942 it was proposed that the two 'Fuso' class battleships should be converted to the hybrid battleship/aircraft carrier standard that was pioneered by the two units of the 'Ise' class, but the plan was abandoned after the Battle of the Philippine Sea in June 1944, when the Japanese lost virtually all of their surviving naval air power capability.

Both the *Fuso* and the *Yamashiro* were sunk by gunfire and torpedoes during the last action in which battleship fired on battleship, namely the Battle of Surigao Strait within the context of the four-part Battle of Leyte Gulf in October 1944.

'Ise' class
(Japan)

Type: Battleship

Displacement: 29,980 tons standard and 32,065 tons full load

Dimensions: Length 683ft 0in (208.2m); beam 94ft 0in (28.65m); draught 29ft 1in (8.86m)

Armament: Twelve 14in (356mm) guns in six twin turrets, twenty 5.5in (140mm) guns in single mountings, four 3.1in (80mm) AA guns in single mountings, and six 21in (533mm) torpedo tubes in six mountings

Armour: 12–3in (305–76mm) belt, 12–8in (305–203mm) turrets, 12in (305mm) barbettes, 6in (152mm) casemates, 21.25in (5132mm) deck, and 12–6in (305–152mm) conning tower

Propulsion: 24 Kansai boilers supplying steam to four sets of Brown-Curtis turbines delivering 45,000hp (33,550kW) to four shafts

Performance: Maximum speed 23kt; radius 9,680nm (11,145 miles; 17,910km) at 14kt

Complement: 1,360

Japan		
Name	Builder	Commissioned
Ise	Kawasaki	Dec 1917
Hyuga	Mitsubishi	Apr 1918

Although they were planned as improved versions of the 'Fuso' class dreadnought battleships, the two units of the 'Ise' class finally possessed so many improvements that they came to be regarded as a separate class. The major change was in the disposition of the main armament, in which the arrangement of the two central turrets was altered from the

arrangement of the 'Fuso' class to a superfiring arrangement amidships, abaft the second of the two funnels. This allowed a shortening of the hull and simplified fire-control through the availability of three groups of superfiring paired turrets. The secondary armament was also altered, the older 6in (152mm) weapons of the 'Fuso' class being replaced by new 5.5in (140mm) guns located farther forward in well-positioned casemated mountings.

Armour and speed were equal to those of the 'Fuso' class ships but, as in most Japanese warships, habitability was

In her final configuration, implemented in 1943, the Ise became a hybrid battleship/aircraft carrier with her after turrets replaced by a moderately large flightdeck. The Japanese naval air arm had virtually no experienced pilots by this time, however, and the ship therefore never carried embarked aircraft.

The two ships of the 'Nagato' class, seen here in the form of the Mutsu, were the world's first battleships with 16in (406mm) main guns, and in the mid-1920s were revised with the forward funnel trunked aft in an effort to keep smoke away from the superstructure of the 'pagoda' foremast.

decidedly inferior to that of contemporary Western ships.

Between the world wars the two 'Ise' class ships were extensively modernised. In 1926–28 a 'pagoda' foremast was installed, two 5.5in (140mm) guns were removed, and two floatplanes were provided, together with the crane required to lift them onto and off the water alongside the ships. The Kure naval yard then implemented a rebuilding programme: *Hyuga* was rebuilt between October 1934 and September 1936, the same programme being applied to the *Ise* between August 1935 and March 1937. The 'pagoda' foremast was increased in size; the hull was increased in length by the extension of the after part of the hull by 25ft 1in (7.64m); the standard displacement was increased to 35,800 tons (*Ise*) and 36,000 tons (*Hyuga*); new machinery was fitted in the form of eight oil-fired Kanpon boilers supplying steam to four sets of Kanpon geared turbines delivering 80,825hp (60,265kW) to four shafts for a maximum speed of 25.3kt and a radius of about 12,500nm (14,395 miles; 23,125km) at 16kt; the armour protection over the machinery and magazine spaces was increased to a maximum 4.7in (119mm) and external torpedo bulges were fitted; and the armament was modified by the elimination of the torpedo tubes and two 5.5in (140mm) guns and by the addition of eight 5in (127mm) dual-purpose guns in four twin turrets and twenty 25mm AA guns in 10 twin mountings.

It was in this form that the two battleships were committed to the Japanese navy's part in the opening phases of World War II in the Pacific. However, after Japan's loss of three aircraft carriers in the decisive Battle of Midway of June 1942, the *Ise* and the *Hyuga* were taken in hand for conversion to hybrid battleship/aircraft carrier standard. In this conversion the two after 14in (356mm) twin turrets gave way to a large hangar intended to house 22 seaplane bombers or conventional dive-bombers launched by a pair of catapults located on the beams of the ships just forward of the flightdeck's forward edge. The armament of the ships in this hybrid form was eight 14in (356mm) guns, sixteen 5in (127mm) dual-purpose guns, one hundred and four 25mm AA guns, and six 4.7in (119mm) 30-barrel AA rocket guns.

The two ships were used as 'decoy' aircraft carriers in the Battle of Leyte Gulf during October 1944, but in fact never operated aircraft in action, since neither warplanes nor pilots were available. Confined to Kure from early 1945, both ships were sunk by US carrierborne warplanes in July of that year. The ships were raised and scrapped after 1946.

'Nagato' class
(Japan)

Type: Fast battleship

Displacement: 32,720 tons standard and 38,500 tons full load

Dimensions: Length 708ft 0in (215.8m); beam 95ft 0in (29.0m); draught 29ft 9in (9.1m)

Armament: Eight 16in (406mm) guns in four twin turrets, twenty 5.5in (140mm) guns in single mountings, four 3in (76mm) AA guns in single mountings, and eight 21in (533mm) torpedo tubes in single mountings

Armour: 12–4in (305–102mm) belt, 3–1in (76–25mm) decks, 12in (305mm) barbettes, 14in (356mm) turrets, 1in (25mm) casemates, and 12in (305mm) conning tower

Propulsion: 21 Kanpon boilers supplying steam to four sets of Kanpon turbines delivering 80,000hp (59,650kW) to four shafts

Performance: Maximum speed 26.75kt; radius 5,700nm (6,565 miles; 10,550km) at 15kt

Complement: 1,333

The Nagato had a full career in World War II, and survived the war to be expended as a target in the Bikini atom-bomb tests of July 1946.

Japan		
Name	Builder	Commissioned
Nagato	Kure NY	Nov 1920
Mutsu	Yokosuka NY	Oct 1921

The two battleships of the 'Nagato' class are of great importance in naval history as they started a new era in battleship design. The ships introduced the 16in (406mm) gun, were very well protected, and were notably fast for ships of their firepower and protection: they were excellent examples of the fast battleship.

The design of the hull was based on that of the 'Ise' class, although the use of the new 16in (406mm) gun meant that the main armament could be reduced in number from 12 to eight without sacrificing any weight of fire: the twelve 14in (356mm) guns in the 'Ise' class ships provided a broadside weight of 17,857lb (8,100kg) while the equivalent weight for the eight 16in (406mm) guns in the 'Nagato' class ships was 17,513lb (7,944kg), and the latter was fired to a greater

range and with more destructive power. In overall terms, therefore, the use of the larger-calibre gun provided a more effective broadside, but also allowed the use of four rather than six main armament turrets with a consequent saving in weight and hull length. The two ships' powerful secondary armament comprised twenty 5.5in (140mm) guns located in 10 single mountings (seven on the upper deck and three one deck higher) on each beam. A control top was sited in the 'pagoda' foremast, the first of these highly distinctive units to be installed on a Japanese capital ship.

The protection was very good, with a notable increase in both the amount and quality of armour by comparison with that of the preceding 'Ise' class. One retrograde feature in the design was perhaps the propulsion arrangement, which used a mix of 15 oil-fired boilers and six mixed coal/oil-fired boilers.

The two ships were undoubtedly the most powerful battleships in the world in the early 1920s, and provided the Japanese navy with an excellent combination of firepower, protection, speed and seaworthiness.

The Nagato *being re-fitted at Yokosuka Navy Yard in May 1936.*

During the 1920s the forward funnel was swept aft at the top in an effort to keep smoke away from the area of the foremast, which itself acquired its true 'pagoda' style from 1924 with the installation of additional command and control positions. In the mid-1930s both ships were extensively rebuilt, the Kure naval yard being responsible for the improvement of the *Nagato* between April 1934 and January 1936, and the Yokosuka naval yards fulfilling the same obligation to the *Mutsu* between September 1934 and September 1936. The rebuilding programme involved a lengthening of the stern in a process that made the overall length 738ft 0in (224.9m); the addition of external bulges along the waterline resulting in a beam of 113ft 6in (34.6m); the provision of a triple bottom; the revision of the propulsion machinery to provide each ship with 10 Kanpon oil-fired boilers whose lesser volume requirement was augmented by the removal of the forward funnel to permit an enlargement of the 'pagoda' mast; and large-scale revision of the armament. In this last revision, the ships were regunned, the main armament now being able to elevate to 43°, raising range from 30,800yds/28,165m (attainable with the previous maximum elevation of 30°) to 40,480yds/37,015m. Two of the 5.5in (140mm) guns were removed, and the others had their maximum elevation increased from 25° to 35°. The 3in (76mm) AA guns were replaced by eight 5in (127mm) dual-purpose guns in four twin turrets, and twenty 25mm AA guns were installed in 10 twin mountings. Each of the ships was also equipped with three floatplanes that could be launched by a single catapult and then recovered from the water by the ship's crane.

The level of protection was also improved: the thickness of the deck armour was increased to 7in (178mm) over the vital spaces, and the barbettes were increased to a maximum thickness of 22in (559mm). Consequently, the tonnage rose by some 6,500 tons, but the additional power meant that speed dropped only marginally, while the use of oil-fired boilers increased range to 8,650nm (9,960 miles; 16,030km) at 16kt.

Both ships were heavily involved in World War II. The *Mutsu* was lost to a magazine explosion in June 1943, but the *Nagato* survived the war, finally being used as a floating AA battery from January 1945 with an armament of eight 5in (127mm) guns and ninety-eight radar-aimed 25mm guns in 16 triple, 10 twin and 30 single mountings. The *Nagato* was expended as a target ship in the Bikini atom-bomb tests of July 1946.

'Yamato' class
(Japan)

Type: Battleship

Displacement: 68,010 tons standard and 71,659 tons full load

Dimensions: Length 862ft 9in (263.0m); beam 121ft 1in (36.9m); draught 34ft 1in (10.39m)

Armament: Nine 18.1in (460mm) guns in three triple turrets, twelve 6.1in (155mm) guns in four triple turrets, twelve 5in (127mm) dual-purpose guns in six twin turrets, twenty-four 25mm AA guns in eight triple mountings, and four 0.52in (13.2mm) AA machine-guns in two twin mountings

Armour: 16.1in (409mm) belt, 9.1–7.9in (231–200mm) deck, 21.5–2in (546–50mm) barbettes, 25.6–7.6in (650–193mm) turrets, 19.7–11.8in (500–300mm) conning tower, and 11.8–3in (300–76mm) torpedo bulkhead

The Yamato and her sister ship Musashi were the world's largest and most powerfully armed battleships, but were built after the day of the battleship had passed.

Propulsion: 12 Kanpon boilers supplying steam to four sets of Kanpon geared steam turbines delivering 150,000hp (111,840kW) to four shafts

Performance: Maximum speed 27kt; radius 7,200nm (8,290 miles; 13,320km) at 16kt

Complement: 2,500

Japan		
Name	*Builder*	*Commissioned*
Yamato	Kure NY	Dec 1941
Musashi	Mitsubishi	Aug 1942

Without doubt the largest and most heavily armed battleships to date, the two completed units of the 'Yamato' class resulted from the preparation of no fewer than 23 designs between 1934 and 1937. The first two of a projected six 'Yamato' class ships were ordered in 1937, for construction under conditions of the utmost secrecy that involved the erection of high fences, protective roofing and camouflage netting. The building dock at Kure was specially enlarged for the *Yamato*, while the *Musashi* was launched from slipway at a weight of 35,737 tons (surpassed only by the liner *Queen Mary*).

Two further 'Yamato' class battleships were ordered in 1939: these ships were the *Shinano*, which was converted into an aircraft carrier during construction and was sunk (on

The two ships of the 'Yamato' class were notable for the great elegance of their line as well as their exceptionally potent armament, which was based on a primary armament of nine 18.1in (460mm) guns in three triple turrets and a secondary armament of twelve 6.1in (155mm) guns in four triple turrets.

her maiden voyage) by a US submarine in November 1944; and hull No. 111 that was scrapped at Kure in 1941–42 when only 30 per cent complete. Plans in 1942 for the standard 'Yamato' class No. 797 and also for No. 798 and No. 799, which were each to mount six 20in (508mm) guns, were soon abandoned.

The *Yamato* had a bulbous drag-reducing bow, considerable beam, and a relatively shallow draught of the type suitable for movement in Japanese coastal waters. In an effort to make the protection as effective as possible, the propulsion machinery was accommodated in a length representing only 54 per cent of the ship's waterline length. The main armour deck could withstand anything up to a 2,200lb (998kg) armour-piercing bomb dropped from 10,000ft (3,048m). Below this deck on each side, 16.11in (409mm) side armour – sloping outward at 20° and able to withstand an 18in (457mm) shell at 23,000–32,000yds (21,000–29,300m) – ran down for some 63ft (19.2m) to a 7.9–3in (200–76mm) anti-torpedo bulkhead, which itself sloped down at 14° to the outer plates of the double bottom and extended fore and aft as a 3–2in (76–51mm) screen beneath the magazines.

The three main armament turrets, each carrying three 18.1in (460mm) guns, had an individual weight of 2,774 tons, and each gun fired up to two 3,240lb (1,470kg) shells per minute to a range of 45,290yds (41,400m) at a maximum elevation of 45°. The three 50ft (15.24m) rangefinders for the main armament (later supplemented by fire-control radars) were located on top of the streamlined cylindrical tower that replaced the 'pagoda' foremasts of other Japanese capital ships. Later changes in the armament scheme of the *Yamato* included the replacement of the two 6in (152mm) triple turrets on each side of the single funnel amidships by an additional twelve 5in (127mm) dual-

purpose guns in twin turrets. The ship's final light AA armament in 1945 comprised one hundred and forty-six 25mm guns in 40 triple and 26 single mountings.

The Yamato was finally expended in an attempt to reach Okinawa, where the ship was to have beached herself as an unsinkable battery against the American invasion.

The Yamato had a specialised anti-aircraft armament of no less than one hundred and fifty 25mm cannon.

Although they were fine seaboats and ships of great aesthetic appeal, the *Yamato* and the *Musashi* had wholly undistinguished combat careers, primarily because of the Japanese naval high command's reluctance to hazard the ships without air cover (which Japan could not provide after the middle of 1942). In fact, when the ships were used without air cover, both were sunk by air attack. The *Musashi* took between 11 and 19 torpedo hits and at least 17 direct bomb strikes before sinking in the Battle of the Sibuyan Sea during the Battle of Leyte Gulf. The *Yamato*, heading a task group on a one-way 'suicide mission' to Okinawa to oppose the American invasion in April 1945, was intercepted in the East China Sea by US carrierborne warplanes and fell to between 11 and 15 torpedo hits and at least seven direct bomb strikes.

'Tennessee' class
(USA)

Type: Battleship

Displacement: 32,300 tons standard and 34,000 tons full load

Dimensions: Length 624ft 6in (190.7m); beam 92ft 3in (29.7m); draught 30ft 3in (9.2m)

Armament: Twelve 14in (356mm) guns in four triple turrets, fourteen 5in (127mm) guns in single mountings, four 3in (76mm) AA guns in single mountings, four 6pdr guns in single mountings, and two 21in (533mm) torpedo tubes in single mountings

Armour: 14–8in (356–203mm) belt, 5–2.5in (127–64mm) decks, 13in (330mm) barbettes, 18–9in (457–229mm) turrets, and 16in (406mm) conning tower

Propulsion: Eight Babcock & Wilcox boilers supplying steam to two sets of Westinghouse turbo-alternators powering four electric motors delivering 30,910hp (23,045kW) to four shafts

Performance: Maximum speed 21kt; radius 8,700nm (10,020 miles; 16,100km) at 10kt

Complement: 1,083

USA			
Name	No.	Builder	Commissioned
Tennessee	BB-43	New York NY	Jun 1920
California	BB-44	Mare Island NY	Aug 1921

Although modelled closely on the two battleships of the preceding 'New Mexico' class, the two ships of the 'Tennessee' class had a number of important differences, most notably the first use of turbo-electric drive in a complete class and the movement of the secondary

Above: *Second unit of the 'Tennessee' class, which was a repeat of the 'New Mexico' class with a new armament layout, the California was little altered before the Japanese attack on Pearl Harbor, in which the ship was sunk. Salved and reconstructed in 1943, the ship gained anti-torpedo bulges, new secondary and tertiary armament, a massive single funnel, and a tower foremast for service in the Pacific as an aircraft-carrier escort and shore bombardment type.*

Seen in the earlier part of her career, the California was typical of the American battleships designed before and during World War I in having a pair of very distinctive cage masts that were light yet very rigid and therefore well suited to the installation of director control positions for the main armament.

armament to a higher level than in earlier American dreadnought battleships.

These were the last US battleships with 14in (356mm) main guns, and this armament was located in four centreline triple turrets installed as fore and aft superfiring pairs. The turrets could maintain a rate of three salvoes per minute, and the broadside weight was 16,800lb (7,620kg). While the ships of the 'New Mexico' class had a numerical advantage in their secondary armament (22 compared with 14 5in/127mm guns), their secondary battery was inferior in qualitative terms as it was located in hull casemate mountings, where it could not be worked in any sort of sea.

The use of turbo-electric propulsion was a bold step, as the heavier machinery required more space and needed careful insulation, but it offered advantages such as removing the need for separate reversing turbines, and allowing rapid change from ahead to astern drive. In overall terms, however, the ships were undoubtedly slow by contemporary standards.

In 1924 two guns were removed from the secondary armament, the torpedo tubes were removed, and the anti-aircraft armament was increased. In 1929–30 provision was made for the shipping of reconnaissance and gunnery-spotting floatplanes through the installation of two catapults (one on 'X' turret and the other on the quarterdeck), the

The Tennessee was built mainly in World War I for completion in June 1920, and was badly damaged at Pearl Harbor in December 1941 but was rebuilt for recommissioning in May 1943. The ship then served extensively in the Pacific, where she was damaged by kamikaze attack in April 1945, and was finally decommissioned in February 1947 before being scrapped in 1959.

stepping of aircraft-handling derricks from the main mast, and the positioning of a crane on the stern. Few other changes were made in the ships before World War II, when both ships were damaged in the Japanese attack on Pearl Harbor in December 1941.

The ships were then reconstructed with a revised dual-purpose secondary armament, which by 1945 comprised sixteen 5in (127mm) L/38 guns controlled by four specialised high-angle/low-angle director control towers as well as an anti-aircraft battery that included 40mm Bofors guns (40 or 56 in 10 or 14 quadruple mountings in the *Tennessee* and the *California*) and 20mm Oerlikon cannon (48 or 52 in single mountings in the *Tennessee* and the *California* respectively). Other changes included the removal of the aircraft catapult from 'X' turret, the stepping of light pole masts fore and aft, the addition of extensive radar for search and fire-control purposes, the thickening of the main and lower deck armour to 5 and 4in (127 and 102mm) respectively, and the addition of external bulges that increased the beam to 114ft 0in (34.75m): these changes increased the displacement to 37,000 tons.

Both vessels served extensively in the Pacific theatre until the end of World War II, in the course of which the ships survived *kamikaze* attacks during the early part of 1945. The ships were 'mothballed' after the war and were sold for scrap in 1959.

'Colorado' class
(USA)

Type: Battleship

Displacement: 31,500 tons standard and 33,590 tons full load

Dimensions: Length 624ft 0in (190.2m); beam 97ft 6in (29.7m); draught 29ft 9in (9.1m)

Armament: Eight 16in (406mm) guns in four twin turrets, fourteen 5in (127mm) guns in single mountings, four 3in (76mm) AA guns in single mountings, four 6pdr guns in single mountings, and two 21in (533mm) torpedo tubes in single mountings

Armour: 16–8in (406–203mm) belt, 14in (356mm) bulkheads, 3.5–1.5in (89–38mm) decks, 14in (356mm) barbettes, 18–5in (457–127mm) turrets, and 18–8in(457–203mm) conning tower

Propulsion: Eight Babcock & Wilcox boilers supplying steam to two sets of Curtis (*Maryland* and *West Virginia*) or Westinghouse (*Colorado*) turbines powering electric motors delivering 27,200hp (20,260kW) to four shafts

Performance: Maximum speed 21kt; radius 10,000nm (11,515 miles; 18,530km) at 10kt

Complement: 1,119

USA			
Name	*No.*	*Builder*	*Commissioned*
Colorado	BB-45	New York SB	Aug 1923
Maryland	BB-46	Newport News	Jul 1921
West Virginia	BB-48	Newport News	Dec 1923

Although it was a virtual repeat of the 'Tennessee' class, the 'Colorado' class differed in design from its predecessor mainly in having revised armament. Each of the ships was still

The Maryland was a member of the 'Colorado' class, which was built during and after World War I as a counter to Japanese construction. The design was basically an improved version of the 'Tennessee' class, with the earlier type's twelve 14in (356mm) guns in triple turrets replaced by eight 16in (406mm) guns in twin turrets.

fitted with four turrets in fore and aft superfiring pairs, but whereas the 'Tennessee' class had carried three 14in (356mm) weapons in each turret, the 'Colorado' class had two 16in (406mm) guns in each turret. The *Colorado*, *Maryland* and *West Virginia* were all completed quite rapidly in the immediate aftermath of World War I, but the *Washington*, third unit of the class and launched by New York Shipbuilding in September 1921, was overtaken during completion by the Washington Naval Treaty and cancelled in February 1922. The unfinished ship nonetheless played an important part in American naval developments, the hull being used for research into explosions and blast before finally succumbing to hits from 14in (356mm) shells in November 1924.

The three completed ships were modernised in 1928–29, the major alterations being the removal of the underwater torpedo tubes, the installation of extra AA guns, and the addition of handling equipment and catapults for floatplanes. Further modernisation was undertaken between 1939 and 1941: two 5in (127mm) guns were removed, and additional light AA guns were shipped. Radical alterations were effected during World War II, the *Maryland* and the *Colorado* receiving similar modifications. External bulges increased the beam to 108ft (32.9m), the cage main masts were shortened and replaced by control towers, and the AA armament was boosted: by 1945 the *Maryland* had a new secondary armament (replacing the original secondary and tertiary armaments) of sixteen 5in (127mm) L/38 dual-purpose guns in eight twin turrets, and a dedicated AA armament of forty-eight 40mm Bofors guns in 12 quadruple mountings and forty-four 20mm Oerlikon cannon in single mountings: these secondary and dedicated AA armaments were controlled by two specialised high-angle/low-angle director control towers. The *Colorado* had her secondary armament reduced to eight 5in (127mm) L/51 guns in single mountings, but the AA armament comprised eight 5in (127mm) L/38 dual-purpose guns in twin turrets plus forty 40mm Bofors guns in 10 quadruple

The Colorado was undergoing a refit at the time of the Japanese attack on Pearl Harbor in December 1941, but returned in 1942 for service throughout most of the Pacific campaign of World War II. Two further refits were undertaken in this period, the first cutting down the main mast and increasing the anti-aircraft armament, and the second replacing the stump main mast with a tower mast and altering the secondary and AA armament. The ship was decommissioned in January 1947 and scrapped in 1959.

The Maryland was completed in July 1921, and in World War II survived bomb hits at Pearl Harbor as well as a torpedo strike in 1944 and two kamikaze attacks in 1944 and 1945, before being decommissioned in April 1947 and scrapped in 1959.

mountings and thirty-seven 20mm Oerlikon cannon in single mountings. Both ships also had additional horizontal armour, and in concert with the other changes this raised the full-load displacement to 39,000 tons in the *Maryland* and 40,395 tons in the *Colorado*.

The *West Virginia* was sunk during the Japanese attack on Pearl Harbor, but was salvaged and repaired, and by 1944 she was basically similar to the ships of the 'Tennessee' class with large external bulges increasing the beam to 114ft 0in (34.75m) and the secondary and AA armaments revised to include sixteen 5in (127mm) L/38 dual-purpose guns in eight twin turrets, sixty-four 40mm Bofors guns in 16 quadruple mountings, and eighty-two 20mm Oerlikon cannon in a mix of quadruple, twin and single mountings, all controlled by four specialised high-angle/low-angle director control towers.

The *Maryland* and the *Colorado* were scrapped in 1959, and the *West Virginia* was scrapped in 1961.

'North Carolina' class
(USA)

Type: Battleship

Displacement: 38,000 tons standard and 46,770 tons full load

Dimensions: Length 728ft 9in (222.12m); beam 108ft 4in (33.02m); draught 32ft 11.5in (10.04m)

Armament: Nine 16in (406mm) guns in three triple turrets, twenty 5in (127mm) dual-purpose guns in twin turrets, sixteen 1.1in (28mm) AA guns in four quadruple mountings, and twelve 0.5in (12.7mm) AA machine-guns

Armour: 12–6.6in (305–168mm) on 0.75in (19mm) belt, 14.7–16in (373–406mm) barbettes, 16–7in (406–178mm) turrets, 5.5–5in (140–127mm) deck, 11in (279mm) bulkheads, and 16–14.7in (406–373mm) conning tower

Propulsion: Eight Babcock & Wilcox boilers supplying steam to four sets of General Electric geared steam turbines delivering 121,000hp (90,220kW) to four shafts

Performance: Maximum speed 28kt; radius 17,450nm (20,095 miles; 32,335km) at 15kt

Complement: 1,880

USA			
Name	No.	Builder	Commissioned
North Carolina	BB-55	New York NY	Apr 1941
Washington	BB-56	Philadelphia NY	May 1941

The two battleships of the 'North Carolina' class were the first American capital ships built after the ending of the limitations on ship size and main armament calibre imposed by the Washington Treaty in 1922. In its original design, however, the type observed the limitations imposed by the London Naval Treaty (1936), which specified a main armament calibre of no more than 14in (356mm). When Japan refused to ratify this treaty, the American designers then replaced the planned 14in (356mm) quadruple turrets with 16in (406mm) triple turrets, and these turrets were then fitted on all subsequent US battleships. The weight of the more powerful armament resulted in a 2kt loss of speed, but the level of inbuilt protection, which had been planned to counter fire only up to a maximum of 14in (356mm), nevertheless proved adequate in service.

The armoured main deck ran into the upper edge of the outward-angled main belt, which was 16ft 0in (4.88m) deep and extended to the forward and after barbettes with a narrow rearward strake running to the stern. Especially good protection was provided for the steering gear, which had 11.75in (298mm) side, 11in (279mm) fore and aft bulkhead, and 6in (152mm) overhead armour. Protection against torpedoes was also comprehensive, and comprised external bulges along the waterline and three longitudinal bulkheads extending vertically to the lower deck.

The main armament comprised nine 16in (406mm) guns, each capable of firing a 2,700lb (1,225kg) shell to a maximum range of 36,900yds (33,740m) at its maximum elevation of 45°. These nine guns were installed in three triple turrets in the form of a superfiring pair forward and a singleton aft. The secondary armament of twenty 5in (127mm) dual-purpose guns was concentrated amidships in 10 twin turrets, and on the quarterdeck were two catapults and a crane for use by three floatplanes. By 1945, the tertiary armament for the anti-aircraft role had been altered from the scheme listed in the above specification, to ninety-six 40mm Bofors guns in 24 quadruple mountings and thirty-six 20mm Oerlikon cannon in the *North Carolina*, or sixty 40mm Bofors guns in 15 quadruple mountings and fifty-six 20mm Oerlikon cannon in the *Washington*.

During World War II both ships saw extensive service in the Pacific; on 15 November 1942, the *Washington* and the *South Dakota* sank the Japanese battle-cruiser *Kirishima* off Savo Island in the Solomons group. The *Washington* was sold and scrapped in 1960–61 but the *North Carolina*, which was stricken in June 1960, is preserved as a memorial in the State after which she was named.

'South Dakota' class
(USA)

Type: Battleship

Displacement: 37,970 tons standard and 44,520 tons full load

Dimensions: Length 680ft 0in (207.26m); beam 108ft 2in (32.97m); draught 35ft 1in (10.69m)

Armament: Nine 16in (406mm) guns in three triple turrets, sixteen 5in (127mm) dual-purpose guns in eight twin turrets, twenty 1.1in (28mm) AA guns in five quadruple mountings, and twelve 0.5in (12.7mm) AA machine-guns

Armour: 12.2in (310mm) on 0.875in (22mm) main belt, 17.3–11.3in (439–287mm) barbettes, 18–7.25in (457–184mm) turrets, 6–5.75in (152–146mm) deck, 11in (279mm) bulkheads, and 16–7.25in (406–184mm) conning tower

Propulsion: Eight Babcock & Wilcox boilers supplying steam to four sets of General Electric geared steam turbines delivering 130,000hp (96,930kW) to four shafts

Performance: Maximum speed 27.5kt; radius 15,000nm (17,275 miles; 27,795km) at 15kt

Complement: 1,793

USA			
Name	No.	Builder	Commissioned
South Dakota	BB-57	New York SB	Mar 1942
Indiana	BB-58	Newport News	Apr 1942
Massachusetts	BB-59	Bethlehem	May 1942
Alabama	BB-60	Norfolk NY	Aug 1942

In the 'South Dakota' class ships the designers and the US Navy had accepted a number of indifferent features (most notably reduced habitability and a degree of blast

interference between the 5in/127mm dual-purpose gun turrets and the lighter AA mountings) so that speed and offensive power could be maintained on a hull shortened by some 50ft 0in (15.2m) by comparison with the preceding class, and in order that improved horizontal and underwater protection could be worked into the hull.

The most notable characteristics of the 'South Dakota' class ships were the provision of only a single funnel that was faired into the after part of the bridge, and the widening of the 1.5in (38mm) weather deck almost to the hull sides so that the 5in (127mm) dual-purpose battery was carried one deck higher. Three aircraft, for which two catapults and a recovery crane were carried, were embarked for reconnaissance and gunnery-spotting purposes.

The side armour was internal, sloped down at an angle of 19° from the heavy armour deck, and extended to the double bottom as a pair of longitudinal anti-torpedo bulkheads. Outboard of this belt armour was a large anti-torpedo bulge subdivided on either side by three longitudinal bulkheads. A 0.625in (16mm) splinter deck of mild steel lay only 2ft 7in (0.8m) below the main armour deck. Among the other protective features was a so-called 'tunnel' stern, in which the substantial skegs of the outboard propellers were designed to provide additional protection against torpedoes.

The main armament layout was the same as that of the

The Alabama was the fourth of four 'South Dakota' class battleships completed in 1942 to a design that was based on that of the 'North Carolina' class, with shortened length to allow for an improvement in protection without an increase in displacement.

'North Carolina' class, and differences between the four ships of the 'South Dakota' class included a revised secondary armament of twenty 5in (127mm) dual-purpose guns in 10 twin turrets on the last three ships, a propulsion arrangement with eight Foster Wheeler boilers supplying steam to four sets of Westinghouse geared steam turbines (in the *Indiana* and the *Massachusetts*), and provision for the *South Dakota* to operate as a force flagship with an elevated conning tower. (Requiring a sacrifice to save topweight, it was this feature that resulted in the secondary battery of this ship being reduced from 10 to eight 5in/127mm twin turrets.)

It was originally planned that each ship would be fitted with a tertiary armament of twelve 1.1in (28mm) AA guns in three quadruple mountings, but all the ships were eventually fitted with a heavier anti-aircraft battery that included between forty-eight and seventy-two 40mm Bofors guns in 12–18 quadruple mountings plus between fifty-six and seventy-two 20mm Oerlikon cannon.

All four battleships saw very extensive service in World War II, which they all survived, and were decommissioned in 1946–47. Schemes for their updating or conversion to alternative roles proved abortive, and *South Dakota* and *Indiana* were sold and scrapped in the early 1960s; *Massachusetts* and *Alabama* are kept as memorials in the States after which they were named.

'Iowa' class
(USA)

Type: Fast battleship

Displacement: 44,560 tons standard and 55,710 tons full load

Dimensions: Length 887ft 2.5in (270.4m); beam 108ft 2.5in (33.0m); draught 38ft 0in (11.6m)

Armament: Nine 16in (406mm) guns in three triple turrets, twenty 5in (127mm) dual-purpose guns in 10 twin turrets, sixty 40mm Bofors AA guns in 15 quadruple mountings, and sixty 20mm Oerlikon AA cannon in single mountings

Armour: 12.25in (311mm) belt, 11–8.5in (279–216mm) bulkheads, 6–0.5in (152–12.7mm) decks, 17.3–1.5in (439–38mm) barbettes, 19.5–7.25in (495–184mm) main armament turrets, 1–0.75in (2–519mm) secondary armament turrets, and 17.5–16in (445–406mm) conning tower

Propulsion: Eight Babcock & Wilcox boilers supplying steam to four sets of General Electric geared steam turbines delivering 212,000hp (158,065kW) to four shafts

Performance: Maximum speed 33kt; radius 18,000nm (20,725 miles; 33,355km) at 12kt

Complement: 1,921

USA			
Name	*No.*	*Builder*	*Commissioned*
Iowa	BB-61	New York NY	Feb 1943
New Jersey	BB-62	Philadelphia NY	May 1943
Missouri	BB-63	New York NY	Jun 1944
Wisconsin	BB-64	Philadelphia NY	Apr 1944

The Iowa *was the lead vessel of a four-ship class that was arguably the best if not the largest or most powerfully armed battleship family of all time.*

The Iowa and her sister ships were notable for their superb balance of firepower and protection on a long hull capable of speeds unsurpassed by other battleships.

Late in 1936, and believing that Japan would refuse to ratify the London Naval Treaty, the US Navy started work on the design of a new class of fast battleship to succeed the 'South Dakota' class currently being built. The failure of the London Naval Treaty meant that battleship displacement increased to a limit of 45,000 tons, and the Americans decided to use the tonnage now permitted for extra power and protection rather than for additional or more potent gun armament. The maximum possible beam was desirable but was limited to a size that could be accommodated by the Panama Canal, so the additional displacement was used in a lengthening of the hull, and this resulted in a higher length/beam ratio that in itself offered significant advantages in the achievement and maintenance of higher speed. The additional volume provided by the longer hull was used for a more powerful propulsion arrangement, and with an additional 70,000hp (52,190kW) from the new machinery the ships of the 'Iowa' class could easily attain 33kt, which made them the fastest battleships ever built.

Although the armament was not increased in terms of calibre or number, it was improved radically by the adoption of a new 16in (406mm) main gun: this was an L/50 rather than an L/45 weapon, and the weapon fired its projectile at a higher muzzle velocity for greater range and accuracy. Three of these improved weapons were installed in a new turret, which was some 190 tons lighter than its predecessor without any loss of internal volume or protection. The secondary armament remained unaltered at twenty 5in (127mm) dual-purpose guns in 10 twin turrets located as five turrets on each beam. The tertiary armament for the anti-aircraft role was originally planned as thirty 3in (76mm) guns in 15 twin turrets, but early World War II campaigns in Europe had indicated that larger volumes of smaller-calibre fire were more effective for the protection of point targets, so the tertiary armament was altered to large numbers of 40mm Bofors and 20mm Oerlikon weapons. In the *Missouri* and the *Wisconsin*, this

light anti-aircraft armament eventually totalled eighty 40mm
Bofors guns in 20 quadruple mountings and forty-nine
20mm Oerlikon cannon.

The protection was planned on the same scale as that of
the 'South Dakota' class, but was more carefully designed.
From the lower edges of the main belt, 1.5in (38mm) armour
extended down to the turn of the bilges, and the design was
given effective internal protection rather than external anti-
submarine protection. Internally, the armour consisted of four
thick longitudinal bulkheads, with the alternate bulkheads
reaching up to the armoured main deck in order to provide
wing compartments. The two main armour decks ran into the
top and bottom edges of the main belt. In overall terms,
therefore, an increase of 200ft (61m) in length and 10,000
tons in displacement yielded a design that was very fast and
exceptionally well protected, and admirably suited to the
battleship's definitive World War II role, which was the escort
of aircraft-carrier groups and shore bombardment rather
than surface combat against other battleships.

The *Iowa* and the *New Jersey* were ordered in 1938 as
the first pair, *Missouri* and *Wisconsin* following in 1939 as the
second pair. The *Illinois* and the *Kentucky* were planned as
the third pair in 1940, but neither of these was completed:
the *Illinois* was cancelled in August 1945 when only about

20 per cent complete, and the *Kentucky* was launched in January 1950 without machinery and was then scrapped. The *New Jersey* was very similar to the *Iowa* apart from her machinery and her complement of sixty-four rather than sixty 40mm guns; the *New Jersey* was also 3in (7.6cm) longer and 3in (7.6cm) wider in beam than the *Iowa*. The second pair of ships followed the first pair at the same yards, and likewise had different machinery; the pair also had a lighter full-load displacement, and a revised tertiary armament with an increased number of 40mm Bofors guns and a reduced number of 20mm Oerlikon cannon. By the end of World War II, all four battleships of the 'Iowa' class had individual radar-controlled directors for their 40mm Bofors mountings.

The ships were placed in reserve during the late 1940s, were recalled to first-line service for the Korean and Vietnam Wars, and were recommissioned in the 1980s as platforms for a hybrid mixture of heavy guns, Tomahawk surface-to-surface cruise missiles, Harpoon anti-ship missiles, helicopters and VTOL warplanes before final decommissioning in the late 1980s and early 1990s.

The New Jersey *was the second unit of the 'Iowa' class to be completed, and in World War II saw extensive service in the Pacific theatre from 1943 to the end of the war as one of the escorts for the US Navy's fast carrier task forces.*